MW01277421

THIS IS
REAL
Life

THIS IS REAL

REAL

Life

Sylvia Hall

MAURICE BASSETT

books for athletes of the mind

This Is Real Life: Love Notes to Wake You Up

Copyright 2018 by Maurice Bassett

Maurice Bassett
P.O. Box 839
Anna Maria, FL 34216

Contact the publisher:
MauriceBassett@gmail.com
www.MauriceBassett.com

Contact the author:
www.sylvia-hall.com

Cover design by Carrie Brito
Layout by Chris Nelson

ISBN: 978-1-60025-125-2
Library of Congress Control
  Number: 2018906767

For Elias and Olive

"If a thing loves it is infinite."
~ *William Blake*

this is real life

so,
how can you wake up?
knowing
right now
everything you need
to proceed with ease
and excitement
and wholehearted gratitude
resides within you
this very moment,
now

all it was

and then
all at once
she realized—
the virus
she had contracted
was indisputably
a common case
of normalcy
and the cure,
it turned out, was
increasing
her daily dose of
creativity

connect the dots back

i have no interest
in motivating you.
that's heavy lifting.
hard work
that rarely works.
i'm here
rather
to inspire you.
to remind you
really
of what you already know.
to reawaken,
quite simply,
your desire.
to connect the dots
back
to your highest self

catch and release

the free-spirit within knows
to catch and release her dreams.
it is her divine nature

wild

my hair is big
and I am wild
and I like it.
my heart is
so full
it aches.
and I know—
we are loved.
beyond any good reason.
i've discovered
there need be
no reason.
it's simply how
we are
designed.
preformatted
with love.

collide

the light
of inspiration
is magnetic
and contagious.
it's where passion
and purpose
collide.

lift

lift the illusion
that something is missing
and
embrace
the space of
possibility

move

move your body
to free your mind—
kick loose
the illusionary
leash of worry—
distance yourself from struggle
and lack
and urgency.
move your body
and
watch it all
move
away
from
you.

love yourself

love yourself
little by little.
don't catastrophize
yet
love yourself,
each little entity
unconditionally
little
by
little,
now.

this?

so what if
this is it?
can you find
a way
to be okay
with
"just" this?

luminosity

she became
obsessed
with light.
lightness.
daylight.
the sun's
golden glow.
lamps.
lampshades.
light bulbs,
and the like.
soaking in
every bit
of brightness
her heart
expanded
in exponential
voltages

downspout

she cried
in the shower
and somehow
felt relieved
to see
all
the
drops
going
down
the
same
downspout

enchant the bridge

someday
you will discover a
way
to enchant the bridge between
the *you*
who is divinely connected
to everyone and everything—
and the *you*
who is a one-and-only,
who is inhabiting
a body
in this world
as a human being
on a soul's
experience
of a lifetime.

any given moment

in any given moment
are you prepared
to ask yourself:
"how
can I
make
this
more
fun?"

somewhere

somewhere between
the day-to-day busyness
and
the simultaneous boredom,
there is a magic
to be experienced.
do you dare
to illuminate
that bridge?

gratitude

swimming in gratitude
proves to be a quantum
exercise for the soul

contentment prayer

quiet
my mind
and
fill up
my heart.
amen

staying awake

waking up,
it turns out—
can happen
instantaneously.
seamlessly
and effortlessly.
staying awake,
however,
is more complicated.
what if, then,
we could
commit
to waking up
again and again
until

waking up and staying awake

became

one and the same?

utterly aching

maybe the pain
is too much.
achingly relentless
borderline unbearable.
but maybe, too,
you are stronger
than you know.
and perhaps
feeling the depth of such raw and real
and charged emotion
is what's evolving you
into an even more
beautiful and expansive
human being

feel free

feel free, darling
to be who you wish to be
and
show up as you wish to be seen.
create
with wild abandon
and
embrace
the uncommon experience
of sincere
self-expression
as if your life
depended upon it.

burn it all up

burn up every
to-do list.
stop. with. all. the. doing.
let
it
all
go
with a deep breath
and a simple knowing.
it's all
already yours
always, already yours
anytime and every time
you are willing to
let it in.

these questions

pause
and ask yourself:

who am I
really?

why am I here?

and what do I really want for this
day?

and yet,
please—
do not answer these questions
within the limited confines of your
mind,
that place which is overrun and
distorted—

instead,
fall deeply into these questions and

notice the answers which
come up from inside of your
heart
space.

much lighter

if you can hold a breath in
for a moment
and then
release
everything,
all of it,
and
let
every
heavy
thing
go,
you might be surprised
how much lighter
you feel.

notice

notice
what is
and
what isn't
on your
"to feel list"
today

on purpose

what kind of
thoughts
would you like to
think
on purpose?

every ache

every ache
we have
is an ocean
of chance
to alleviate
some
unnecessary
suffering

the page

i'll let the page heal me
word by word
i'll remember
that my thoughts can
construct a problem
or create
momentary bliss
with just as much
concentrated effort

right now

when you find yourself
swimming
incessantly
in thought after thought after
thought—
ask yourself:
is this really
a problem
i need
to solve
right
now?

every one

every step
a kiss to the earth
and every skyward
glance an invitation
for divine consummation

collector

i've written myself silly
collecting
all of the reasons why today is
perfect

then, swimming
in all of the succulent possibility

go grab a notebook and a pen
get in on this

become this kind
of collector with me

it's twisted

untangle
yourself
from worries
which
make
life
feel
so
heavy.
open yourself up
to the radiant possibility
of a life that is
supposed to be
fun.

plummet

if you could
plummet
deeply
into a perfectly felt trust
of your uniquely
distinct purpose,
how would that
alter your vision?

you can

you can
expand
without
chasing
and
you can
experience
relief
without
settling

within, without

there is infinitely
more within
than there ever
will be
without

are you willing?

are you willing to be
like a fully inflated,
colorfully
vibrant
beach ball,
basking
on a half-melted
patch of leftover
snow?

just thoughts

it was never you.
it was always me
and my ideas
about you.

ripples

if every
inner-thought
creates a ripple
in our
outer-space,
it begs the question:
in what sort of
ripples
do you
want to swim?

just for the sake of it

what you offer
to this day
matters.

how brilliantly
can you shine…

just for the sake
of your own radiance?

again and again

again and again
and again
we will be faced
with the lesson that says:
the truth will set you free.
how many times
do we have to keep
relearning this lesson
before it sticks
for good?

authenticity means

not just
going with the flow,
but
being
your
very
own
flow.

what if?

what if
you could
fall in love
with the
entire sky
or even just
one
single
cloud?

do this

gift yourself
the enchantment
of total inner fulfillment.
it's a magic
only you
can create.

fears

watch your fears
go up in flames
when gratitude
fills your bones

what is it?

you don't have to have
one million and one
dollars, or a boomin' and bustlin'
dream-come-true business.
you don't have to
absolutely
love your job,
or for that matter,
your life
at this particular moment...
yet, i do
lovingly encourage you
to fully know the answer to the
question:
"what is it that really
lights me up?"

giving up

i used to be so good,
following all the rules—
doing what was
expected.
until one day
recently,
i realized:
the rules
were not made in my favor.
and now?
i'm following my heart
instead of the rules.
i'm giving up good
for great.

About the Author

Sylvia Hall is the cofounder of Lifted, a wellbeing movement. She lives in Kansas City with her family of two kids, two dogs, and one husband. Sylvia loves all things creative and is wildly optimistic about our capacity to feel better. You can find out more at:

www.sylvia-hall.com

Publisher's Catalogue

The Prosperous Series

#1 The Prosperous Coach: Increase Income and Impact for You and Your Clients (Steve Chandler and Rich Litvin)

#2 The Prosperous Hip Hop Producer: My Beat-Making Journey from My Grandma's Patio to a Six-Figure Business (Curtiss King)

* * *

Devon Bandison

Fatherhood Is Leadership: Your Playbook for Success, Self-Leadership, and a Richer Life

Sir Fairfax L. Cartwright

The Mystic Rose from the Garden of the King

Steve Chandler

37 Ways to BOOST Your Coaching Practice: PLUS: the 17 Lies That Hold Coaches Back and the Truth That Sets Them Free

50 Ways to Create Great Relationships

Business Coaching (Steve Chandler and Sam Beckford)

Crazy Good: A Book of CHOICES

Death Wish: The Path through Addiction to a Glorious Life

Fearless: Creating the Courage to Change the Things You Can

The Prosperous Coach: Increase Income and Impact for You and Your Clients (The Prosperous Series #1) (Steve Chandler and Rich Litvin)

RIGHT NOW: Mastering the Beauty of the Present Moment

Shift Your Mind, Shift the World: Revised Edition

Time Warrior: How to defeat procrastination, people-pleasing, self-doubt, over-commitment, broken promises and chaos

Wealth Warrior: The Personal Prosperity Revolution

Kazimierz Dąbrowski

Positive Disintegration

The Philosophy of Essence: A Developmental Philosophy Based on the Theory of Positive Disintegration

Charles Dickens

A Christmas Carol: A Special Full-Color, Fully-Illustrated Edition

James F. Gesualdi

Excellence Beyond Compliance: Enhancing

*Animal Welfare Through the Constructive
Use of the Animal Welfare Act*

Janice Goldman

*Let's Talk About Money: The Girlfriends' Guide
to Protecting Her ASSets*

Sylvia Hall

This Is Real Life: Love Notes to Wake You Up

Christy Harden

*Guided by Your Own Stars: Connect with the
Inner Voice and Discover Your Dreams*

*I Heart Raw: Reconnection and Rejuvenation
Through the Transformative Power of Raw
Foods*

Curtiss King

*The Prosperous Hip Hop Producer: My Beat-
Making Journey from My Grandma's Patio
to a Six-Figure Business (The Prosperous
Series #2)*

David Lindsay

*A Blade for Sale: The Adventures of Monsieur
de Mailly*

Abraham H. Maslow

The Psychology of Science: A Reconnaissance

Being Abraham Maslow (DVD)

Maslow and Self-Actualization (DVD)

Albert Schweitzer

Reverence for Life: The Words of Albert Schweitzer

William Tillier

Personality Development Through Positive Disintegration: The Work of Kazimierz Dąbrowski

Margery Williams

The Velveteen Rabbit: or How Toys Become Real

Colin Wilson

New Pathways in Psychology: Maslow and the Post-Freudian Revolution

Join our Mailing List:

www.MauriceBassett.com

MAURICE BASSETT

books for athletes of the mind

Made in the USA
Columbia, SC
31 August 2018